ESTRENO Collection of Contemporary Spanish Plays

General Editor: Phyllis Zatlin

VANZETTI

LUIS ARAÚJO

VANZETTI

(Based on the personal correspondence of Bartolomeo Vanzetti)

Translated by Mary-Alice Lessing

ESTRENO Plays
New Brunswick, New Jersey
1999

ESTRENO Contemporary Spanish Plays 16
General Editor: Phyllis Zatlin
              Department of Spanish & Portuguese
              Faculty of Arts & Sciences
              Rutgers, The State University of New Jersey
              105 George Street
              New Brunswick, NJ 08901-1414 USA

Library of Congress Cataloging-in-Publication Data
Araújo, Luis, 1956-
    Vanzetti
    Translation of: Vanzetti
    Contents: Vanzetti
    1. Araújo, Luis, 1956- Translation, English
I. Lessing, Mary-Alice. II. Title.
Library of Congress Catalog Card No.: 98-73881
ISBN: 1-888463-08-2

© 1999 Copyright by ESTRENO Plays

Original Play © Luis Araújo, 1996
English Translation © Mary-Alice Lessing, 1999
First Edition

All rights reserved.
Except for brief passages quoted in newspapers, magazines, radio or television, no part of this publication may be reproduced or transmitted in any form or by any means, electronic or mechanical, including photocopy, recording, or by an information storage and retrieval system, without permission in writing from the publisher.

Published with support from
Consulate General of Spain in New York

Cover: Jeffrey Eads

A NOTE ON THE PLAY

The play, *Vanzetti*, by Luis Araújo, as translated by Mary-Alice Lessing, explores the true story of Sacco and Vanzetti and the tensions that exist in a democratic society between its ideals, and the compromise of those ideals by the realities of the capitalist impulse and the exploitation of its workers.

Utilizing only three actors, the play develops its themes and moves toward its preordained conclusion. The play embraces some of the elements of a Greek tragedy as its protagonist, Bartolomeo Vanzetti, tempts the Fates. The audience is aware early on in the play that Vanzetti's passionate commitment to justice and his opposition to the "system" will result in his downfall. Bartolomeo's inflexibility and *hubris* in the context of the hostile political environment of the 1920s where there was great fear of the stranger and the immigrant, all conspire to lead to his destruction. Only it is not the gods on Olympus that he antagonizes, but the industrialists and power-brokers who are threatened by his revolutionary rhetoric and passion on behalf of the downtrodden. Add to this a politically ambitious judge and a conspiring district attorney who are willing to pervert the justice system, and the stage is set for the inevitable tragedy.

Interestingly, the playwright does not attempt to resolve the issue of whether Sacco and Vanzetti were guilty of the charges brought against them, an issue that remains unsolved to this day. Rather, he deals with compelling themes such as the nature of self-sacrifice, and the isolation of the man who demands that society look squarely in the mirror and judge whether it is living up to its moral foundations.

Ultimately, the play is an exploration as to what degree a free society will accommodate the agitator within its midst.

This is an intelligent and thought-provoking play that will challenge audiences in the same manner that Vanzetti challenged members of his society and time. The play moves though various environments from Italy to the United States, and courtroom to prison, and affords a theatre the opportunity of great flexibility in staging the work.

Gabor Barabas, Executive Producer
New Jersey Repertory Company

Luis Araújo
Photo: Antonio Cabañas

ABOUT THE PLAYWRIGHT

Luis Araújo (b.1956) is one of Spain's bright young dramatists whose plays, *Las aventuras y andanzas del Aurelio y la Constanza* (1983) ("Tony and Abigail Sail the High Seas"), *Fantastic Calentito* (1986), *La parte contratante* (1992) ("The Contracting Party") and *Vanzetti* (1993) have met with great public acclaim in Spain. *Vanzetti* in translation has also been staged in France and Portugal. He has written successful works for television and radio as well.

As an actor, author, artistic director and scriptwriter, he has worked with many theatrical companies in Spain. In France, he has collaborated with such luminaries as Jean Louis Barrault, Madeleine Renaud and Pierre Chabert in presenting dramatic works.

Araújo's talents are not limited to stage performance and production. For the past six years he has served either as Secretary General or vice-president of the Asociación de Autores de Teatro de España (Spain's dramatists'guild). He has written and lectured on the art of playwriting and has directed numerous workshops featuring the plays of other Spanish writers. As a professor of acting, translation and playwriting, he has taught in Spain, Canada and Belgium.

In writing *Vanzetti*, Araújo drew from letters written by Bartolomeo Vanzetti to his sister in Italy to create a drama as compelling in its tragedy today as it was in 1927 when justice seemed to bow to the political, social and economic pressures of the time.

Mary-Alice Lessing

CAUTION: Professionals and amateurs are hereby warned that *Vanzetti*, being fully protected under the Copyright Laws of the United States of America, the British Empire, including the Dominion of Canada, and all other countries covered by the Pan-American Copyright Convention and the Universal Copyright Conventions, and of all countries with which the United States has reciprocal copyright relations, is subject to royalty. All rights, including professional, amateur, motion picture, recitation, public reading, radio and television broadcasting, and the rights of translation into foreign languages, are strictly reserved. Particular emphasis is laid on the question of readings, permission for which must be secured in writing.

Inquiries regarding permissions should be addressed to the author through:

SGAE
Fernando VI, 4
28004 Madrid
Spain
Phone: 34-91-349-96-86
Fax: 34-91-349-97-12

or through the translator:

Mary-Alice Lessing
27 Marion Rd.
Princeton, NJ 08540
Tel. 1-609-924-3534

Vanzetti was first staged at the Cuarta Pared Theatre in Madrid on October 26, 1993. Produced by C.C.C.K., it was directed by Luis Araújo.

Vanzetti has been translated to Portuguese and French. It received its Portuguese-language premiere in Porto, Portugal in July 1995, under the direction of Acácio de Carvalho. The first French-language production was created by the Compagnie Thalie of Nantes in April 1998, in cooperation with Amnesty International.

Happiness, dear sister, is the only sound and ethical state of being. Everything else may be what you want it to be, but not health nor happiness. I wouldn't know how to explain myself briefly on this particular subject. On the other hand, I do know that you have to convince yourself.

Bartolomeo Vanzetti

CHARACTERS

BARTOLOMEO VANZETTI	A militant union member and anarchist. An immigrant.
LUIGIA VANZETTI	His sister.
WEBSTER THAYER	The judge.
FATHER	The father of Luigia and Bartolomeo. A merchant.

PLAYWRIGHT'S NOTE

Webster Thayer and Father are to be played by the same actor.

TRANSLATOR'S NOTE

The letters on which this text is based, compiled by Vincenzina Vanzetti and Cesare Pillon, were published under the title, *Vanzetti, Cartas desde la prisión*, Barcelona: Granica Editor, 1976.

(As the lights come up, BARTOLOMEO VANZETTI is standing looking in silence at the horizon. There are various pieces of furniture around the set. LUIGIA VANZETTI runs on stage with a letter from her brother. She opens it and reads.)

LUIGIA: August 23rd, 1917.
BARTOLOMEO: You know I have only one pair of shoes, so when I have to take them to be repaired I'll be barefoot because my old ones are no good anymore. Please send me a new pair, if you can, or get someone here to buy them for me, whatever seems best to you. If you have them made over there, ask for a big size.

(LUIGIA shouts waving the letter.)

LUIGIA: Papa! Papa! A letter from Bartolomeo!

(FATHER appears with a shoebox in his hand.)

FATHER: You know I need someone to take care of the business with me. At my age I can no longer look after storage, shipping, and the wine and fruit sales without someone's help. If you wanted to, without any effort, you could have right here all the things that are costing you such enormous sacrifices over there. Bartolomeo, my son, are you sure you don't want to give it a try? Why ruin your life working for others when you could run your very own business here?

(FATHER hands the box to LUIGIA.)

LUIGIA: Leave him alone, Papa. He's old enough to know what he's doing.

(LUIGIA hands the box to BARTOLOMEO, who gives her another letter. She opens it immediately and starts to read. Meanwhile, BARTOLOMEO opens the shoebox and exchanges the shoes for the old ones he is wearing.)

FATHER: I have to hire strangers while my son is trying to fix up the world in a country where even the biggest imbecile can make a fortune.
BARTOLOMEO: Make a fortune? Only the banks make fortunes. They invest astronomical sums in poor countries and then force them to set up governments that will bring them a better return. Fortunes are made, in whatever way possible, by the boundless ambition of a few vultures who are ready to suck the blood from any poor souls who are broken and defeated. Big fortunes have their beginnings in wars, in increases in poverty, in public riots that are crushed bloodily, and in great waves of emigration. The law of might has always made right.

Cristian Casares, Carlos Kaniowsky, and Encarna Breis in original production of *Vanzetti*. Cuarta Pared, Madrid, 1993. Dir. Luis Araújo

(FATHER changes into JUDGE WEBSTER THAYER and begins to play golf, unaware of BARTOLOMEO.)

LUIGIA: You are so pig-headed. It's right that makes might, not the other way around.

BARTOLOMEO: Being right, or believing you are, can give an individual or a society the courage and power needed to achieve great deeds, including even heroic death. But nothing more. Who can be sure that he is right? Each of the countries at war at this moment thinks that it is right and that it has justice on its side--which is impossible. That's the clearest proof that no society or individual knows even relatively where right lies. If we knew that, there would be no more wars.

THAYER: Right! Right! To hell with this right business! When has a worker lived the way he does today? How have we stirred up this country, Katzmann? Do you think they're going to make their working conditions better by going on strike and closing the factories?

LUIGIA: January 12th, 1919.

BARTOLOMEO: As you have learned from my letters, when I arrived in this country it was being destroyed by a tremendous crisis.

THAYER: Palmer is right. If one of those agitators had fallen opportunely from the fifteenth floor of the courthouse, we wouldn't find ourselves threatened today by that mob. Anyone can have an accident. But these gutless politicians don't have the balls to send those who are starving to death back to their own country. There's no room in this country for decent people anymore. *(He hits a good drive which lights up his whole face.)* Seventeen holes! How about that! And they say I'm getting old. Leave them to me and you'd see those foreigners walk the straight and narrow. A person comes here to work. If someone wants to dream up a philosophy, let him go study the great thinkers in Berlin. *(He hits another drive.)* I'm on the eighteenth green, Katzmann! You owe me a dinner!

LUIGIA: Tell me about the United States. I get excited just thinking that you may have seen the Statue of Liberty and the skyscrapers. Are they really as impressive as they look on the postcards? I picture you strolling along among them in your new shoes. You must be the best-looking man in New York. What do the girls wear? Do you like one of them?

BARTOLOMEO: I've met people of every nationality imaginable. At times I've been really miserable, feeling that I'm in the midst of strangers who are indifferent, even hostile. I've had to put up with the scorn and insults of people whom I would have cut down to size, if I could have spoken their language one tenth as well as I speak my own.

LUIGIA: You must write me more. Can't you see that I'm dying of curiosity to know about everything?

BARTOLOMEO: I found work right away in a hotel chain and for ten months I didn't have too many problems. Then I spent two months with Giacomo Caldera and afterwards another eight months in a French restaurant where I learned a little of that language. But I couldn't stand it. Maybe because I was feeling sick or maybe because I can't put up with anything that seems unfair to me, I left New York and came up here to this part of the country. *(BARTOLOMEO pulls out a bundle of pamphlets and a revolver from under his clothes. He puts them in the shoebox, which he hides.)* I've done some farming, gone logging in the woods, worked in some brick factories, dug ditches and worked in a stone quarry. Later I was hired by a baking company and most recently I've been working for another company, installing telephones.

LUIGIA: It makes me sad to think that you'll fall in love with an American and you'll never want to come back to Villafalleto. But I console myself thinking that it is God's will and I am sure that, come what may, He will do what's best for you. Papa sends you a great big hug and wants to know if there is anything you need.

(Two gunshots are heard, screams, running footsteps, a car rushing away. THAYER walks over to the shoebox, picks it up off the floor and looks inside it.)

BARTOLOMEO: There are a lot of foreigners here who never do any work. They don't do anything but have a good time and get all dressed up. They belong to secret organizations and make a living from the crimes they commit. I'm almost always alone. The immigrants that I meet are, for the most part, pretty uneducated. I don't know what to talk about with them.

THAYER: For the last time, Andreu Salsedo, who asked you to print those pamphlets?

BARTOLOMEO: Don't get the idea that this is a civilized country. The people around here have some fine qualities and it's fascinating to see the cosmopolitan mix in the streets; but, if you take away their money and their fashionable clothes, you'll find that they are semi-barbarians, fanatics and criminals.

THAYER: We know you were going to get together Sunday in Brockton. Who paid you for the printing? You're going to tell us right now, or you'll never talk again, not in my language nor in yours.

(Sounds of a struggle between several people are heard, some shouts, a window being opened, some punches, and finally a long drawn-out scream from someone falling through space, followed by a dull thud.)

BARTOLOMEO: Public justice is based on brute force and for the poor alien who tries to assert his rights they have invented police weapons, jail and the penal code.

THAYER: Arrest Nicola Sacco and Bartolomeo Vanzetti.

(Police sirens are heard traveling along the streets.)

BARTOLOMEO: Here you're only worth something if you make money. It doesn't matter if you steal or kill for it. A lot of people have made a fortune informing on fellow workers or their own friends. Human dignity isn't worth a cent. The only moral code is the law of the jungle. In the midst of all this evil I've managed to remain true to myself and I haven't been forced to stoop to any dirty business. Up until now no policeman has laid a finger on me as a criminal.
THAYER: Arrest Nicola Sacco and Bartolomeo Vanzetti.

(He becomes FATHER again.)

BARTOLOMEO: When we were arrested the police found some underground pamphlets on us and a short manifesto calling for a meeting which was to have taken place the Sunday after our arrest. I was supposed to speak at that meeting. I had written the manifesto in the car during our trip. It was crucial and Nicola Sacco had to get it to Salsedo to have it printed. Sacco was carrying his pistol, and I had an old revolver which had been given to me when I got to New York, so we could protect Salsedo.
FATHER: Tell me the truth, son, tell me exactly what happened. What did you have to do with Andreu Salsedo? How many times have I told you to come home? When you get out of this mess take the first boat back. You know that you'll never want for anything here and I *(Short pause.)* I'm getting old, son. I pray God you haven't done anything really foolish. I'm sure that everything will turn out all right soon. Do you need money?
LUIGIA: April 15th, 1920.

(FATHER has turned back into THAYER, who is assembling a cot out of some pieces of wood.)

THAYER: We've got two armed robberies without any charge. There were no victims in the first one in Bridgewater. But today's in South Braintree has left us with two men dead, gunned down in the middle of the street, Frederick Parmenter and Alessandro Berardelli, the paymaster from a shoe factory and his guard. Whoever it was got away with the company's entire payroll of $15,776. We've got six bullets from a .38. That's all we have. If we keep on like this, they're not going to let us get any sleep, even at home. The press is beginning to make a lot of noise demanding those responsible, Palmer. I think you'd better come up quickly with a court hearing for those two dead men. Talk with Katzmann. Bring me some evidence.

LUIGIA *(Sitting down at the foot of the cot)*: Why have you been arrested? Did you have a fight with someone?

BARTOLOMEO: Anyone who hopes to have himself chosen for high positions has to prove by his actions that he is capable of doing anything so long as it serves some *(Pause.)* great cause.

LUIGIA: Was it because you ran off to Mexico during the conscription?

BARTOLOMEO: Palmer, the Attorney General, talked absurdly when he took charge. That's how he started a wave of terror aimed at foreigners, accusing them of subversion. He began with a fierce campaign in the newspapers denouncing any kind of plot to overthrow the government and its institutions. He painted a picture of imminent danger from an apocalyptic revolution.

LUIGIA: Was it because of the pamphlets?

BARTOLOMEO: Since brainwashing brought him good results, he moved on to action. He violated the privacy of homes and personal correspondence, invaded offices, newspaper bureaus, political groups. He made arrests and detained hundreds, persecuting and torturing them. He made false accusations and held them incommunicado and even deported great numbers of them.

LUIGIA: Suppose they throw you out of the country now, after all you've gone through to make your own way.

BARTOLOMEO *(Falling onto the cot)*: Many times when I'm out at sea, at work or off on long hikes, I shut myself away from my surroundings and my thoughts are filled with you. How many doubts, how many hopes, how many serious reflections about you come to mind! I'm your brother, Luigina, and truly your happiness is more important to me than my own.

LUIGIA: Papa walks around dejected all day with a vacant look and he doesn't attempt to talk with people.

BARTOLOMEO: In the Brockton Police Station, they put us on exhibit to the town for a whole week.

LUIGIA: But what do they accuse you of?

BARTOLOMEO: Palmer's secretary at that time was a man named Louis Post. He published a book about that scandalous situation, documenting all the atrocities that were committed: the individuals who were driven crazy, the suicides, the murders, the families that were torn apart, the innocent people who were convicted or deported.

LUIGIA: But what were you doing with a revolver in your pocket?

BARTOLOMEO: We were arrested right at the end of that wave of terror. Palmer was publicly attacked by some prominent people. A highly respected lawyer explained to what extent Palmer had violated the Constitution and the Penal Code, concluding that every honest citizen should be ashamed at what he succeeded in doing in the name of the law. Those dangerous conspiracies never existed; but Palmer spent, on his newspaper campaign alone, more than two million dollars from the Treasury to get the support of public opinion.

LUIGIA: Fine. You don't have anything to do with it. The political situation justifies everything.

BARTOLOMEO: It was our arrest that gave him the chance to justify his conduct. Even the police overstepped all the state and federal laws by collaborating in the indictment against us.

LUIGIA: Yes, of course, you're a victim. Everyone is against you. Aren't you speaking out against plots like those of that man Palmer? Do you expect to make me believe that the whole world has ganged up on you? After all, who are you that the District Attorney and the Chief of Police would waste any time getting rid of you?

THAYER: Bartolomeo Vanzetti, stand up.

LUIGIA: Why won't you tell me what it is that you've done?

THAYER: You are accused of participating in the armed robbery attempt which took place in the town of Bridgewater, in the Commonwealth of Massachusetts, on the 24th of December, 1919. In consideration of the evidence against you and the guilty verdict handed down by the jury, you are hereby condemned by the Superior Court of Plymouth this day, the 16th of August, 1920, to a minimum term of twelve years in prison and a maximum of fifteen to be served in the State Prison at Charlestown.

LUIGIA: Is this how you propose building a world that is more just, through violence and crime? Bartolomeo, is that really your idea of justice?

BARTOLOMEO: My idea of justice? Do you know what justice is? Do you know whom the laws protect? *(Silence. The sounds of factories.)* They call Youngstown "The City of Smoke" because there are several giant steel mills there that spew forth fire and smoke like volcanoes, day and night without stopping. From far off the city looks as if it were under an immense black umbrella.

THAYER: The war in Europe gave such a boost to the steel industry that the city thrived and drew thousands upon thousands of workers until it became a virtual human anthill.

BARTOLOMEO: Thanks to the sweat of those people, a few speculators forgot that saying, "If you go out too far on a limb, it may break." And it did break a little, two years ago--just a little.

THAYER: Two hundred homes burned like paper and the factories went up in flames.

LUIGIA *(Sighing)*: And a few policemen were sent straight to glory.

BARTOLOMEO: While people were burning up their faces and lungs on the job, in eight months' time a single factory gave out thirty million dollars to its stockholders. Thanks to that marvelous war in Europe some people out there became millionaires.

LUIGIA: Does that mean that they should be robbed of what they earn through their investments and their jobs? Do you think it's easy for them to build factories, manage production and organize their marketing? Do you know how many workers are left destitute each time a business fails? Do you know how much money one of those investors loses each time a factory closes? What would your friends live on if there weren't people who could set up those factories? Furthermore, anyone who honestly works can prosper and start his own business. That's how the great countries have gotten to be what they are.

BARTOLOMEO: Absolutely, you're right! The wonderful progress of the workers! Five or six years ago, they earned enough with their jobs to get ahead; now they're earning twice as much and it's not enough. Their wives are working, too, and at the end of the month with two paychecks it comes out the same. There is hardly enough for them to meet the normal family problems.

LUIGIA: So what do you propose? Killing? Stealing? Robbery as a social plan to guarantee justice? Is that what you propose?

BARTOLOMEO: I've knocked down mountains, cleared forests and built mansions, only to end up not owning a single thing. That's the story of my life. Do you understand? I've seen how man's ambition and selfishness poison every mouthful of food, defile and break the laws of nature, encourage crime and sow the seeds of hate and corruption. I've seen how man's ambition and selfishness doom the majority of mankind to all sorts of misfortune, humiliation and squalor.

LUIGIA: Bravo! Well done. I think your speech is stupendous. So now you are in jail and I have to live with your father who has shame written all over his face.

(Silence.)

BARTOLOMEO: When Papa talks to you, raise your head and look him straight in the eyes.

FATHER: My son, I believe in you as nobody ever can. I only want you to tell me that I'm not mistaken.

(BARTOLOMEO hands his FATHER a letter which he and LUIGIA read.)

LUIGIA: Charlestown, Massachusetts, October 1st, 1920.

FATHER: "Dear Father, I've held back from writing you until today because I was hoping all the time, from one day to the next, that I could give you good news. But things are going badly, and, in light of that, I've come to a decision. I know how sad this situation must be for you and for all my family and that is precisely what hurts me most. I encourage you all to be strong, as I am, and to forgive me the hurt which I, unwittingly and through no fault of my own, am causing you."

BARTOLOMEO: I know several people have written you but I don't know if you have received everything, since many of the letters and newspaper clippings sent

by my friends to people and groups over there have never reached them. All of which makes me think that the authorities are censoring any correspondence related to my case.
FATHER: "A friend brought me your greetings and assured me that you are convinced that I am innocent."

(LUIGIA and her FATHER look silently at each other. Then they continue reading.)

BARTOLOMEO: Yes, I am innocent and, in spite of everything, I'm well and I'm doing whatever I possibly can to keep my health. You must know now that...
LUIGIA: "I am accused of murder!"

(LUIGIA takes the letter away from her FATHER. Six loud gun shots are heard. There are screams, sounds of running, the squeal of tires. FATHER becomes THAYER. LUIGIA continues reading.)

LUIGIA and BARTOLOMEO: "I haven't killed, injured or robbed anyone ever, but, if they do the same thing they did in the other trial . . . "
THAYER: Witnesses, Katzmann, all you need are witnesses. Someone who may have seen them in South Braintree on April 15th. His accomplice's revolver is a .38 and those six bullets are from a .38. It shows that he was in Braintree that night.
BARTOLOMEO: I've been accused, along with Sacco, of having killed two men. I hardly know that city. The plan laid out by District Attorney Katzmann with the judge's approval went along at full speed. But I had never been in that city. They knew they had nothing against me for this new charge, just as they had nothing for the first one.
THAYER: The jurors in the second trial will know that he is already serving a sentence. If we try the two of them together. *(Pause.)* Talk to the jury about what's going on, damn it. Two foreigners are two foreigners. Everyone knows that they're the ones that are turning this country upside down. Look what happened in Chicago. The public wants the men who are guilty. They're fed up with legal red tape. These two are agitators, anarchists. Haven't you read that shit they had on them when they were caught? This sea of undesirables will end up throwing us out of our offices, and, if we don't cut them off sharply, they will throw us off our streets and out of our cities. Those good-for-nothings have no religion, no education, no morals. The people are shouting, asking for his hide. The next election will be a walk in the park for anyone with the guts to give them what they're looking for.

(Silence. BARTOLOMEO dreams, tossing and turning on the cot.)

BARTOLOMEO: They're coming to get me. They're coming to get me. *(Short pause.)* No! They're crazy. *(Pause.)* They're in uniform? *(Pause.)* Let go of me. *(Pause.)* Why? *(Pause.)* You can't. I'm innocent. *(Pause.)* For protection? *(Pause.)* I'm a foreigner. *(Pause.)* You can't; it's my revolver. *(Pause.)* For money? That's a lie! You're crazy. *(Pause.)* Why does he say that? I don't know him. I swear it. I don't know him. Nicola, you tell him. *(Pause.)* Where's my revolver? *(Pause.)* They can't. They're coming, they're coming. Nicola, here they come. *(Pause.)* Only a few? *(Pause.)* I love you. Help me. Help us. *(Pause.)* They know it; they know it, Luigina. Look. Look at them. They're shouting. They're crying out. They're asking for my freedom. *(Pause.)* Father, Father! Don't you see them? You should feel proud, Father; you should feel proud! Father? *(He sits up suddenly in the cot.)* I hope my friends over there won't deny me their cooperation; but I don't feel safe. I don't feel safe.

LUIGIA: Who are your friends here?

BARTOLOMEO *(Wide awake)*: Two deputies from the Italian Parliament have taken an interest in my case. In addition to the workers in Italy, like Malatesta and others, the workers in Mexico, Spain and France are mobilizing in my defense and they're contributing money. Last Sunday a letter arrived which said that two hundred thousand workers in New York were solidly behind me. You can't kill a person today for defending liberty and justice.

FATHER: These days you can't kill a person for defending liberty and justice.

LUIGIA *(To the audience)*: You can't kill a person these days for defending liberty and justice?

FATHER: This is ridiculous; in a democracy there are systems for the control of government. How could the abuses of ages past be committed today? The Inquisition doesn't exist; you can't burn a modern-day Galileo. And if abuses are committed, you only need to bring the case before a judge.

LUIGIA: And who passes judgment on the judges?

FATHER: There are petitions, appeals, Superior Courts. The possibility of such an abuse by a magistrate is absolutely remote. They can't make decisions on their own.

LUIGIA: But they can join forces with other judges, take advantage of the way opinions are going and make use of political interests and newspaper campaigns.

FATHER: Make use of them how? Do you think that just because workers go on strike they can be convicted of armed robbery and murder? Do you think the judges are crazy? Even if their interests and ideas are opposed to the accused, do you think they have sufficient power to get rid of him with any kind of excuse whatsoever? They need evidence, Luigina, evidence to prove guilt. Material evidence--I don't know what sort--like the gun that was fired, the motives that drove him, the witnesses that saw him do it. How in the world could they rig all that so they could do away with someone?

LUIGIA: They can find false witnesses and fix the trial.

FATHER: Why, in heaven's name, would a Massachusetts judge want to kill a Vanzetti?

LUIGIA: Bartolomeo is an agitator, Papa. Everyone knows that.

FATHER: I was in that country thirty years ago. At that time it was the most liberal country that I could have known. There were people from all over the world, every religion, every ideology, race and custom imaginable. *(Pause.)* I'm talking about thirty years ago. *(Sounding doubtful.)* I can't believe that today they could . . .

LUIGIA: Could kill an innocent man! Isn't that what you were going to say? It frightens you to think that because he's your son.

FATHER: They don't accuse a man of murder because he's distributing pamphlets!

LUIGIA: But they do, if they're trying to get rid of someone who is becoming too much of a nuisance to them with his political agitation. Bartolomeo has stirred up the workers. He has ranted at them in their factories. He has made them realize that their situation is little less than slavery. He has instigated meetings, rallies, demonstrations, strikes. He's raised the dignity of people who believed that they had no defense against the men who control the money and the power and he's brought them face to face with *(Hesitantly.)* against those who . . .

FATHER: Against those of us who exploited them. Isn't that what you were going to say? Bah!

(Silence. FATHER moves away from LUIGIA.)

LUIGIA: Papa. Papa! Wait!

(FATHER moves off. He becomes THAYER and once again starts puttering, transforming the cot this time into a platform.)

BARTOLOMEO: I said to myself, "I offer you liberty, justice and intelligence, your arms and your heart." That's what I told myself and that's the way it has been. I'm not the young smart aleck that I was. I've become a proud and thoughtful man and I see so much ugliness, so much injustice! I've become a man who fights with all his energy this society of lambs and wolves. I'm ready, without fear or doubts, to throw myself into the battle which is about to begin. That is what nature and destiny have chosen for me.

LUIGIA: Bartolomeo, wait!

BARTOLOMEO: I have witnesses for my defense and I'll fight with all my might. This has always been a desperate fight and one that is unequal when it comes to the ammunition.

(Music of strident improvisational jazz. THAYER has climbed onto the platform and addresses the audience.)

THAYER: The Commonwealth versus Nicola Sacco and Bartolomeo Vanzetti. Gentlemen of the jury . . .

BARTOLOMEO *(To the audience)*: I want to tell you and all my family something else. Don't cover up my arrest. Don't keep it a secret. I am innocent and you have nothing to be ashamed of. Don't be silent. Shout to the four winds, to everyone, that they committed a crime against me; they did it, at my expense, to save the reputation of the police, because it was tarnished by a hundred scandals and failures. The police have been unable to find a single guilty person in the midst of this sea of corruption; but they have succeeded in jailing an innocent person by supporting the hierarchy and authority of an old man--an old man who needs my liberty and my life so he can climb the ladder of success! Don't be silent. Don't ever be silent, because shame is covered up in silence.

LUIGIA: They can't convict you a second time.

BARTOLOMEO: I am innocent! No matter what the results of this trial, I shall continue to be innocent. I'm going to fight like a wild animal until justice is done in my case.

THAYER: Gentlemen of the jury: I have before me a revolver. The Mafia, crimes, law and order, aliens, our homes, our families, our jobs, social upheaval, delinquency, drugs, a peaceful life, atheism, alcohol, our young people, our taxes, decent people, peace, the future, liberty and democracy.

BARTOLOMEO: The whole world is no longer what it was. We live in sad times, a period of corruption in which power is desperately attacked and desperately defended. We are no longer surprised by the most unbelievable things.

THAYER: Gentlemen of the jury: crime, violence, unemployment, crises, economic growth, principles, respect for the law.

BARTOLOMEO: I was simply doing my job. With all my heart I wanted the wealth of our society to belong to all human creatures, because it is the fruit of everyone's labor. But that doesn't mean that I propose the law of the jungle, nor am I so stupid that I believe that robbery or murder is required to instigate revolution.

LUIGIA: Instigate revolution?

THAYER: Gentlemen of the jury: insurrection, revolt, revolution.

BARTOLOMEO: Great spiritual movements don't require money. What we need is clarity, love, ideas, sacrifice, conscience, instinct, soul. We need greater honesty, greater hope. All those things can be brought to light, sown and cultivated in the human heart without resorting to violence.

LUIGIA: My God and my Lord Jesus Christ . . .
THAYER: Gentlemen of the jury: based on the testimonies and evidence delivered by the prosecution, and with the witnesses that you have heard and the evidence you have seen presented by the defense . . .
LUIGIA: Because of who You are, Lord, and because I love You above all things, I humbly beg You with all my heart . . .
BARTOLOMEO: Nobody has ever convinced me to confuse black with white.
LUIGIA: Innocent.
THAYER: This court requests that the verdict be read.
LUIGIA: Innocent.
BARTOLOMEO: If there's someone who views me adversely, it's because he knows that I despise him and he would like to avoid my glance.
LUIGIA: Innocent, dear Lord, innocent.
THAYER: Guilty.

(Silence.)

LUIGIA: If only you had stayed in Italy.
BARTOLOMEO: I don't believe in the justice meted out by men. The only justice lives in the heart of each human being and no amount of evil will ever succeed in crushing it.
LUIGIA: If you had stayed in Italy, we wouldn't have had to go through any of this.
BARTOLOMEO: You're speaking like a child, Luigina. Human life is so uncertain. It develops in the midst of so much danger, so many *(Pause.)* traps . . .
LUIGIA: Couldn't you have married a girl from Villafalleto and taken care of Papa's business?
BARTOLOMEO: That not even the wisest mortal can tell you an hour ahead of time that this will be good or bad for you.
LUIGIA: What might have happened to you if you'd stayed among us? You would have had children, land, clean air stirring the apple trees in the late afternoon sun.
BARTOLOMEO: If I had stayed in Italy, I could have died in an accident or have ended up killing people in that wonderful, most holy war which enjoyed your vote and your enthusiasm.
LUIGIA: We would all have lived in peace, like always, without worries or problems.
BARTOLOMEO: When have you had a life without worries or problems? Instead of losing yourself in those fantasies, look at reality, try to recognize it, meet it head on and control it.

(Silence. They both look at THAYER on the platform.)

THAYER: The accused will rise.

Carlos Kaniowsky in the role of Bartolomeo Vanzetti.
Madrid, 1993

BARTOLOMEO: My lawyer has had an Italian woman, who works as a court interpreter, arrested.
THAYER: This Court of Justice, convened on this day . . .
BARTOLOMEO: She had asked the Defense Committee, which is supporting Sacco and me, for $50,000. With that money, she said, we would first get rid of our lawyers and then hire for our defense the prosecutor's brother and another lawyer from here who owes me some favors.
THAYER: The 18th of July, 1921, has reached a decision to pronounce judgment . . .
BARTOLOMEO: They could get both of us off free and a part of this money, according to this woman, would be used to buy off the foreman of the jury.
THAYER: Against Nicola Sacco and Bartolomeo Vanzetti . . .
BARTOLOMEO: There is an association, made up of lawyers and judicial authorities, which can get anyone acquitted. A woman in Norwood, who killed her husband, was freed after she paid off this group.
LUIGIA: What filthy business!
BARTOLOMEO: Justice is a common whore! What swine the upper class are!
THAYER: Condemning them to death in the electric chair. Court is adjourned.

(The murmur of a large crowd is heard in the distance.)

BARTOLOMEO: One of the witnesses for the prosecution has confessed to our lawyers that he gave false testimony.
LUIGIA: Papa! Papa! The lawyer has appealed the sentence!

(BARTOLOMEO and LUIGIA take down the platform removing THAYER from his place.)

THAYER: Palmer has been publicly attacked by several congressmen. They have accused him in Congress of having waged a dirty war in his fight against subversion.
BARTOLOMEO: A new witness, who had been forced to flee the country earlier, denied categorically that we were among the group who committed the robbery.
LUIGIA: In Italy close to two hundred newspapers have taken up the case: *L'Umanitá Nova* in Rome, *Avanti* in Milan, *Ondine Nuevo* in Turin, *Il Bollettino della Gente di Mare*, *Umanitaria*. It's become a burning issue.
BARTOLOMEO: In addition to that, a lot of irrefutable testimony can be brought in about the shape of my mustache.
LUIGIA *(Laughing)*: The shape of your mustache?
BARTOLOMEO: Don't laugh. It's true. My mustache played an extremely important part in the first trial.
LUIGIA *(Holding up a newspaper picture)*: It looks phenomenal on you.

BARTOLOMEO: You really think so? *(THEY both laugh.)* Madeiros and another convict have confessed to taking part in one of the crimes for which we have been convicted. They swear that they know who the perpetrators of the other one are.
LUIGIA: We've got it, then, Bartolomeo! All we have to do is put pressure on them to denounce the people who are really guilty.

(BARTOLOMEO begins to erect prison bars around himself.)

BARTOLOMEO: The evidence the defense now has against the real murderers is much more solid than the deceptive material they convicted us with.
LUIGIA: They still haven't turned it over to the judge?
BARTOLOMEO: No. *(The crowd sounds stop. There is a brief silence.)* We are ready to do what's needed to protest our conviction, prove our innocence and gain our freedom. But, if it comes to a question of trying to find the guilty people, as our Defense Committee is now doing, we can't be a party to it. We emphatically refuse to do the job of the police.
LUIGIA: Have you gone crazy?
BARTOLOMEO: Public opinion became convinced of our innocence during the trial. Everyone realized that political and racist interests were responsible for our conviction.
LUIGIA: What does that matter now? Find the murderers and they'll set you free!
BARTOLOMEO: Moreover, the Italian government, under pressure from public opinion, will find itself obliged to intervene in all seriousness. People are mobilizing in Spain, too.
LUIGIA: Why won't you turn the killers over to them?
BARTOLOMEO: To a justice system that fills the jails with innocent, naïve people while it protects and exonerates big-time thieves and murderers?
LUIGIA: You know. *(Pause.)* Do you know who they are?
BARTOLOMEO: A fierce battle against capital punishment is being organized in our name. Many influential people are on our side. We're going to get the death penalty abolished.
LUIGIA *(Pulling away from him)*: You're defending them! You're planning to conceal the real murderers!
BARTOLOMEO: Look, Luigia, when they got this shameless scheme started, not even those police pigs, the district attorney or the judge thought that the entire civilian population would take up our defense. They thought that they could do whatever they wanted with us without anyone getting interested in the matter. And now they're more afraid than ashamed.
FATHER: Luigia! Luigina!
BARTOLOMEO *(Growing progressively more agitated)*: The workers have always been the ones who've raised their voices in a hundred different languages, denouncing to the world the corruption in public administration. It's the workers

who have made the earth shake beneath the feet of the men in power who steal and kill.

LUIGIA: Hush!

BARTOLOMEO *(Excited)*: It's always been the workers who have made those who hide beneath their robes, their crosses and their white gloves come to realize that...

LUIGIA: Don't say it!

BARTOLOMEO *(Continuing to be excited)*: They've come to the end of their rope; that they have committed too many crimes; that, once and for all, the only law will be an eye for an eye and a tooth for a tooth!

LUIGIA: Don't talk!

FATHER: Luigina, come here!

(LUIGIA approaches FATHER. BARTOLOMEO remains shut in his cell.)

FATHER: Your brother is a fanatic. Do you understand? A fanatic. He has never been able to understand that he is causing the upset of the very thing which fed him from the time he was born and that we have built up through generations so that you both could have a life free of problems and worries.

LUIGIA: When have we ever had a life free of problems and worries? Didn't your son find himself forced to go off to look for work in a foreign country?

FATHER: If he had taken charge of our sales, his children wouldn't have had to consider an idea like that today.

LUIGIA: And how many others would have had to do it?

FATHER: Our family has never had to reproach itself for anything.

LUIGIA: How many children of the farmhands who gather our fruit or of the truck drivers who carry it to the market will have to go off to a foreign country to find work so that such an idea may seem ridiculous to your grandchildren?

FATHER: Don't talk such nonsense, Luigina. Most of our day laborers would never be able to get another job; they're Morrocans.

(There is a short silence.)

LUIGIA: That's exactly what they think over there about your son.

FATHER: What is it you want? Would you like them to strike and leave the crops rotting on the trucks? Can you imagine what that would mean to us? Well, that's what your brother has been preaching these last few years!

LUIGIA: For that, is it right that he be condemned to the electric chair?

FATHER: If he hadn't insisted on turning the world upside down, nobody would have paid attention to him other than to respect him.

LUIGIA: He is condemned to death! *(Silence.)*

FATHER: Think of where that boy could have gone.

18 - Luis Araújo

LUIGIA: He is condemned to death, Papa!
FATHER: I hope that God will forgive him for what he has succeeded in doing.
LUIGIA: I hope God can forgive you. *(Silence. FATHER slaps his daughter angrily. Silence.)* May God forgive you.

(Silence. It grows dark as voices rise from a large gathering calling for "amnesty". Then light shines on BARTOLOMEO in his cell and the voices cease. There is a long silence.)

BARTOLOMEO: Some important people are coming to see me, people who, if it weren't for this circus, would never have come near anyone like me, a workman and an agitator. We're living in sad times and it is natural that it should work out like this. Inside ninety out of every hundred people there lies a scoundrel, a coward, a hypocrite or a drifter. If you sow winds, you'll reap whirlwinds. Too many innocent people wait for justice, years and years in jail. I wonder how people can accept institutional justice, believe in it and justify it. Some do it out of ignorance, I suppose, others out of pure dishonesty. Whoever has the misfortune to fall into their hands pays for the sins of the whole world. My dear Luigina, you've heard people say that this is the land of the free, but nowhere in the world does a man fear and distrust another man as much as he does here. In the headquarters of the union the workers call one another brothers, but as soon as they step outside, they act like each others' spies and executioners.

(A long silence.)

LUIGIA: October 20th, 1922.
BARTOLOMEO: I am firmly convinced that I have accomplished an enormously useful job for the future of mankind. *(Silence.)* Life is a mystery and we ought to face it with courage. *(Silence.)* I am afraid. I am so terribly afraid of the world *(Pause.)* that I even think I'm lucky to be locked up within these four walls. *(Silence.)* The human race is sick. The world is incurably ill. And I am afraid.

(A long silence. Then a light shines on THAYER.)

THAYER: The defense is prepared to prove that the bullet that killed the guard could not possibly have been fired by Sacco's gun. They say Vanzetti's revolver was not the one that was taken from the guard. It was a .32 caliber and Vanzetti's was a .38. On top of that, they say the idiots on the jury took five bullets with them to their deliberating chamber, violating the legal rights of the accused!

BARTOLOMEO: It is impossible to describe the new trial which lasted six weeks and in which all the social aspects, interests, hatreds, mentalities and antagonisms were brought together. Well, you already know the results. They want everything kept silent to hide their shame. They hope that people will forget it. They're wrong. They have the power and they may abuse it, but those who are oppressed will never forget.

LUIGIA: March 15th, 1923.

THAYER: Nicola Sacco has been on a hunger strike since the 16th of February. He's as stubborn as a mule; he has decided to get his freedom alive or dead. After three years of confinement he's now been fasting for twenty nine days. He's already very weak and, if he continues, he won't live much longer. It's a question of weeks, even days. There is no doubt that he has lost his mental faculties; he's disturbed by what is happening.

BARTOLOMEO: He's convinced that because of that gesture they'll let him go. His position is totally justified, but it's obvious that he's mistaken.

THAYER: The defense team has petitioned the Defense Committee and Nicola Sacco's wife for the authority to have him examined for an opinion by competent physicians. *(He hands BARTOLOMEO a document to sign.)* We must take measures to save him from death by forcing him to eat.

BARTOLOMEO *(Crumpling up the document and angrily throwing it away)*: I absolutely refuse to give you such authorization! Nicola may be upset--why wouldn't he be?--but he is far from crazy. I demand that the Commonwealth take responsibility for the situation that it itself has caused.

THAYER *(Smiling)*: So, the defense has decided to take the matter into its own hands and has asked the Court to have Nicola Sacco examined by experts. When they have given their opinion he will be taken to a home where he will receive the attention needed to save his life and restore his mental health.

BARTOLOMEO: They have no right! They have no right to do that! Nicola is the master of his own fate! They want to make him live so they can put him in the electric chair! Sons-of-bitches!

LUIGIA: Calm down, for heaven's sake. For the love of God, calm yourself. You won't get anywhere losing your temper.

BARTOLOMEO: They have no right! They had their minds made up to kill us before the trial ever began! No jury would have found a dog guilty of killing a chicken with the evidence they presented against us! The Superior Court wouldn't have denied the appeal, even to a mangy dog!

LUIGIA: Only the Lord our God knows what is good for us.

BARTOLOMEO: That's a lot of nonsense! I wish I could believe in some of your myths, Luigina. I wish someone could explain to us the mystery of our existence.

LUIGIA: Give yourself to God, Bartolomeo. Put yourself in His hands and pray.

BARTOLOMEO: Me, pray? I can't. I pray with actions. But you pray, if praying and believing brings you peace; and pray for me, too, for I can't, even though I am looking life and death in the face.
LUIGIA: Trust in God. He alone knows what He is asking of you. Don't pretend to know more than He does.
BARTOLOMEO: Do you think your faith will save you? The only possible salvation for man is his own life. Life itself is a victory for the one who lives it. Nobody has the right to take it away from him *(Pause.)* nor to make him live it!

(Silence.)

THAYER: Representative La Guardia, who has been the assistant to the Mayor of New York, has offered to become part of the defense team, free of charge! Have they all gone crazy? Are they trying to get votes by letting out of jail the agitators who are on the verge of taking over their businesses? They're bringing this country down! Are we going to let them spit in our face? Go ahead, let them go on with their strikes, their rallies, their higher wages, their increased days off, their fewer work hours. Let them reproduce like rabbits! Soon we'll see our daughters going to bed with the offspring of those immigrants, and then it will be too late for crying.
BARTOLOMEO: A politician cannot destroy a nation, but a nation can destroy a politician.
LUIGIA: God is asking an enormous sacrifice of you, because His love for you is everlasting.
BARTOLOMEO: You can't eliminate historic vengeance unless you destroy the human species.
THAYER *(Stepping up onto the platform)*: They will have to be granted a new trial, Katzmann. In order to find them guilty we would have to kill a man using his revolver. Didn't I tell you to bring me evidence? Or do you want us to end up like Palmer? Sons-of-bitches. I haven't been able to sleep at all tonight. The appeal was denied, do you hear me? It's over. The State Supreme Court? I'll be a Supreme Court judge the day those two are burned like a couple of barbecued ribs!
BARTOLOMEO: Someone has changed the barrel on Sacco's gun. Thompson, our lawyer, told me so.
LUIGIA *(Speaking to THAYER while posing as counsel for the defense)*: You cannot hand down a fair sentence, if you don't first order that one hundred shots be fired with the incriminating gun and then compare the marks on the cartridge case and the shells with those on the bullet taken from the victim's body.
BARTOLOMEO *(To the audience)*: It had proved that the marks it left on the shells were different from the ones left on the bullet that killed the guard.

THAYER: District Attorney Katzmann would like to have the gun checked by a prosecution expert before the one hundred shots are carried out.

BARTOLOMEO: The prosecution expert verified that the barrel on the revolver was not the original one. The defense expert checked and confirmed the same thing. Strange thing! The barrel had been substituted, so the ballistic tests couldn't be done.

LUIGIA: Who changed the barrel?

THAYER *(To the audience)*: Did one of you change the barrel of this gun? Whoever did it speak up; you won't need to furnish witnesses.

LUIGIA *(To Bartolomeo)*: There must have been someone whose job it was to look after the revolver.

THAYER: Let the clerk of the Court of Dedham step forward to make a statement.

BARTOLOMEO *(Imitating the court clerk)*: "I have kept it since the last hearing; I never gave it to anyone connected with the defense but, on various occasions, the district attorney and the prosecution expert asked me for it and they took it away, so I don't know if they handled it." *(Turning back into himself.)* The defense didn't see the revolver again while the prosecution asked for it several times and took it away.

THAYER: The defense expert in the last session also dismantled and reassembled Nicola Sacco's gun and two others of the same caliber and make.

BARTOLOMEO: That operation took place before the Court, on the judge's desk, in the presence of the judge himself and the lawyers for the prosecution and the defense.

THAYER: Afterwards they turned the three guns over to the court clerk.

BARTOLOMEO: Making him swear that he would give them to the prosecution whenever they asked for them.

LUIGIA *(To Judge Thayer)*: If your hypothesis is correct, the barrel of the murder weapon must be on one of the other two guns, and the current barrel on the incriminating revolver must belong to one of those other guns.

THAYER: The prosecution expert says that is true.

BARTOLOMEO: And the defense expert says that it is not. This case has been from the beginning, and will be until the end, simply a skirmish in the eternal war between authority and freedom. *(Pause.)* I don't trust lawyers; I am totally convinced that legal defense is absolutely useless.

THAYER: In view of that, once the death sentence is confirmed in the appeal to the Supreme Judicial Court, this Court reserves the right to decide on the date of the execution. Court is adjourned.

(For a few seconds the murmuring of a large crowd can be heard.)

LUIGIA: You don't trust lawyers, you don't agree with the defense, you don't believe in justice, you don't agree with war, you don't agree with the government, you don't agree with God, you don't agree that criminals should be punished. It doesn't matter to you that Nicola is starving himself to death, nor that your father is sinking into a depression.

(Silence. Slow, solemn tempo.)

BARTOLOMEO: It has been a year now that Papa hasn't answered my letters.
LUIGIA: You still haven't asked yourself why?
BARTOLOMEO: A whole year.
LUIGIA: He's very old, wasting away. He's worn out, Bartolomeo, and weak. It's been such a long time since you've seen him. You wouldn't recognize him. All this is much too hard for him. How would you expect him to accept this? He speaks to no one. He scarcely goes out to the street. He's always irritated and grumbling. He's absorbed with his bills and his invoices, going over them day and night.
BARTOLOMEO: I know very well what you're trying to hide from me, Luigia. I know that you're doing it to keep from hurting me. I understand it perfectly, but I need to see reality face to face and look it in the eye, just as I looked right in the eyes of that judge who bowed his head when he was condemning me to death. Do you think I don't know that Papa renounces me and my principles?
LUIGIA: Your principles? You are an imbecile. Would you like to become a hero? Well, you've already succeeded. You are a hero, brother, they're going to crucify you in the name of social justice while millions of people throughout the whole world are angrily shouting your name in front of the authorities. Tomorrow I shall bury you and Papa with an ocean between you, begging God to forgive you both. Our liberator is dead, long live our liberator! You are an imbecile, Bartolomeo Vanzetti.
BARTOLOMEO: The disinherited of the world, the pariahs, that whole nameless mass has rebelled at last. They're done with "take it or leave it." They have forced the men who were sitting pretty to move over. They've kept the most powerful government in the world on its guard for seven years. That's because those who have no name, the forgotten people, also love, hate and hang on to life, and they have their own justice system opposed to the justice of power. They will not let our death go unpunished! Is that what Papa renounces?

(Silence.)

LUIGIA: He can't understand how you can let yourself be killed, covering up for some murderers. How would you expect him to understand it? How would you expect us to understand it?

BARTOLOMEO: The Governor is swamped right now with pleas for pardon from workers' associations and common people, from religious figures, politicians, scientists. artists, professors and lawyers. They most certainly have understood it and they're supporting us.
LUIGIA: What good are those petitions? How have they helped you? Millions of workers have been demonstrating in Europe and America for seven years to have you set free. You're a celebrity. When they seat you in the electric chair, you'll pass into the history of the Revolution. Good luck! The price you will have paid for it won't have been your life only, as you seem to think, but also your father's.
BARTOLOMEO: I am not responsible for my father's life.
LUIGIA: You are nothing but an animal with no scruples, no morals, no God and no restraints on your ambition. You can ignore your father's dead body in the name of liberty and justice.
BARTOLOMEO: Intellectuals, professors, scientists, educated people from every religion and idealogy: Catholics, Episcopalians, Presbyterians, Quakers, freethinkers, atheists. All the newspapers in the country and, what's more, the majority of the nation, the students in almost all the universities and high schools, all public opinion is leaning in our favor. The illegal cooperation between the federal agents, the State Police and those of the district has raised our cause to federal jurisdiction and into the domain of international law. Until recently Governor Fuller was considering washing his hands of the subject, but our arguments and our evidence are irrefutable when it comes to human reasoning. The Governor has received pleas for pardon from fifty million people. If you can't understand it, and if Papa can't grasp what's going on here, I am not to blame!

(Silence. FATHER appears with an apple, which he drops on the platform. He goes to the shoebox and starts looking for something in it.)

LUIGIA: Maybe they'll free you, Bartolomeo. Maybe, at last, your innocence will be proven. Maybe you have saved the oppressed people of the world, especially those two murderers whom you don't want to betray and who will be eternally grateful to you. In the end you're going to exchange your father's life for theirs.
FATHER: Luigina! Luigina! That devilish girl, where could she have put Cuneo's invoices? I don't know what to say about things in this house. *(Pause.)* This house. *(Long pause.)* They don't seem to be mixed in with my papers. But there are letters and more letters. Do they think that I don't have anything else to do but read letters? Who's going to supervise the shipment of apples to Cuneo? Luigina! The invoices for Cuneo! Good God, what a mess! When has this house ever looked so cluttered? *(Pause.)* There were always flowers in this house, on the table. Bartolomeo brought them from the garden, every day, and now there are only papers, papers everywhere. *(Pause.)* I put them in a jar with fresh water. Luigina!

(BARTOLOMEO and LUIGIA appear as adolescents, playfully running about. LUIGIA takes an apple from the table.)

LUIGIA: Let go of me. You're cheating. We said that the one who picked them first got to eat them.
BARTOLOMEO: If you don't give me that apple, I'm going to put you in prison like a thief.
LUIGIA: I didn't take it away from you; you dropped it. If you want it, you'll have to step over my dead body.
BARTOLOMEO: All right, you asked for it.

(BARTOLOMEO pounces on LUIGIA who hides behind FATHER. Both jostle him.)

LUIGIA: Papa, Papa! Tell him to stand still; the apple is mine.
BARTOLOMEO: I picked it from the tree and she took it away from me.
FATHER: Enough now. Settle down before you end up breaking something. It's hard to believe that you're as old as you are.
LUIGIA: But it's my apple and I'm going to eat it.
BARTOLOMEO: Selfish.
FATHER: Come now, Bartolomeo, let her eat the apple and go get another, if you want one. There are two tons of apples in the barn and you have to fight over that precise one. Go. Right this minute they must be loading the trucks from Cuneo. Go tell Fabrizzio to give you a basket for the house.
BARTOLOMEO: Right away, Papa. *(To Luigia.)* Selfish. *(He starts to run.)*
LUIGIA: Bartolo!

(BARTOLOMEO stops. LUIGIA throws him the apple. He catches it, bites into it and it is rotten. Surprised, they both laugh. FATHER continues rummaging through the shoebox.)

FATHER: Will you tell me where you put the Cuneo invoices?
LUIGIA: They're not there, Papa. Those are letters.
FATHER: Letters, letters. What madness is this keeping all these letters? *(Pause.)* As if they were good for anything. Don't I have enough papers in my office already without keeping all these foolish things people write to us? I don't even know who them. What business do I have with the fishermen's union in Ribadesella, if I don't even know where the devil that is? And this one? The metal workers from *(Pause.)* I can't even read the name. Why do all those people feel compelled to write us?
LUIGIA: We ought to be grateful to them, Papa.

FATHER: Grateful to them? Who is to blame for all this mess? You can take all those letters this minute and burn them in the stove. I don't want to hear the subject mentioned again.
LUIGIA: Yes, Papa.
FATHER: Find me the Cuneo invoices. The trucks are going to leave and I don't even know how much they're taking away this time.

(LUIGIA starts to withdraw with the shoebox. She stops.)

LUIGIA: Papa.
FATHER: What now?
LUIGIA: Do you really want me to burn all of them? His, too?
FATHER: Do what you want, but get them out of my sight. *(LUIGIA leaves.)* And for the last time, damn it, bring me the invoices.

(Silence.)

FATHER: I gave you a trade. I couldn't pay for the university for you, but I did give you a trade. Making pastry was as good an occupation as any other. Who knows, you could have managed to open your own business; using fruit and flour from the family, your costs would have been . . . But there was no work. When your mother died, you were just a little fellow of four. Vincenza was barely walking and I had to get a wet nurse for Ettore. For all those years, you acted like a man. And then, when you sailed for America *(Pause.)* I was so proud of you! My son will succeed in that country for he's strong and healthy, like an oak tree, and he has good arms for making his way in life. He's a good worker and . . . and he's an honest young man. *(Silence.)* Your letters disturbed me. You were wandering from one job to the next, never settling down, not practising your trade and you didn't seemed satisfied with anything. You never found a girl who would make you put down roots anywhere. I used to ask myself, "What does he want? What is he looking for?"
LUIGIA: He is trying to get ahead, Papa, trying to earn a little more. *(Pause.)* And he's well and in good spirits.
FATHER: What were you looking for? My God, what were you looking for with a revolver in your pocket spreading hatred, bothering poor people whose habits don't include looking for revenge? The proletariat of the world! Justice for the oppressed! Let's feed a new world with the guts of those who exploit us! Death and destruction for the good of humanity! Blood, blood, and more blood! What was it that you were looking for? *(Silence.)* The world is sick, Bartolomeo, you were right. It is a cancer that feeds on our very own flesh, on our deepest desires, on our truest aspirations. Yes, you were right, the world is sick. But you failed to understand that you can't remove the tumor with a .38 revolver.

(Silence. LUIGIA opens and reads a telegram.)

BARTOLOMEO: July 27th, 1927.
LUIGIA: "Vanzetti is well and would like to see one of his sisters before the 10th of August, the date on which he is to die, if the governor's decision is unfavorable. Be advised to prepare the family in order to spare them any tragic consequences."

(Silence.)

THAYER: You can't fix up the world with a revolver. That idiot Fuller has kept us in suspense for two months. Do you think a governor can just destroy my seven years of work? If the people shout, let them shout. Let them become hoarse. You can't pardon someone who goes around out there stirring up shit. An investigating commission! Jesus Christ! University pen-pushers and know-it-alls! And the Governor sets them on me so they can keep an eye on my work. Who in the hell around here sees to it that the streets are clean so that he can go for a drive in his official car? Who has the way cleared for him so he can say that we don't act like the people in Illinois? This affair is over, Katzmann; the dogs are barking, there's death in the air. It's finished. Get rid of them as soon as possible. Next week. What's the date today? Katzmann?

(LUIGIA and BARTOLOMEO hug each other for a long time in silence. BARTOLOMEO moves gently away. She clings to him again. He pushes her tenderly to one side and turns to the audience.)

BARTOLOMEO: Gentlemen of the jury, Your Honor: What I have to say is that I am innocent, not only of the murders in Braintree but of the robbery in Bridgewater. Not only am I innocent of those two crimes, but never in my whole life have I robbed, killed, or spilled a drop of blood. That is what I want to say. Ever since I reached the age of reason I have fought to eliminate true crime from the face of the earth. These two hands know all too well that I don't need to kill a man in the middle of the street to get money. I can live all right working with my hands, in fact, I can live very well. I could even get by without a job, without hiring my hands out to anyone. I have had many opportunities to become independent and lead the kind of life you all consider better than one where you earn your daily bread by the sweat of your brow. I have denied myself life's comforts because I consider the exploitation of men unfair. I have refused to make a living from business deals because I believe they involve speculation which is harmful to others. That doesn't seem fair to me so I refuse to get involved. Once again I must say that I am not only innocent of all the charges which are brought against me but I have also fought to eliminate every kind of crime: the crimes which ethics and the law condemn and those which official morality and the law sanction and defend, namely the exploitation of man by man. If there exists any reason for which I am convicted it is that and none other. The leading men of Europe, the best writers, the greatest thinkers and the common people of foreign nations have demonstrated in our support. Is it possible that a few men, members of a jury, have the right to issue a conviction which everybody in the world considers unjust, a conviction which I know is unjust? If there is someone who knows whether that conviction is just or unjust, that someone would be Nicola Sacco or I. You see us here before you, Mr. Thayer. For seven years we have been shut up in prison. No human tongue can describe what we have suffered in those seven years; yet, you can see for yourself, I do not stand trembling before you. Are you aware of that? I'm looking you straight in the eye and I'm not blushing nor am I embarrassed. I am not afraid. There could not have been on the face of this earth a judge who was more unjust, more cruel than you have been with us, Mr. Thayer. *(THAYER begins to build the electric chair.)* We have proved it. Even so, we have been denied a new trial. We know that you have been consciously against us from the beginning, even before you saw us for the first time. Before you saw us you already knew that we were radicals, contemptible dogs in your mind. You showed your contempt for us with all your friends at the Worcester Golf Club. I'm sure that, if all those who know what you said about us had the courage to come here and testify, Your Honor--I'm sorry to say this because you're an old man and my father is an old man like you--Your Honor would be forced to come sit next to us. That would, indeed, be complete justice. *(THAYER has finished making the chair.)* When you sentenced me you said that those crimes were in accordance with my principles. I am sure that you, like District Attorney Katzmann, did whatever was in your power to stir up the hatred of the jurors and their prejudice against us. I would go willingly to the gallows if I could say to all mankind, "Be on your guard. Everything they tell you, everything they promise you is a great lie, an illusion, a deception, an abomination. They promised you liberty; where is liberty? They promised you prosperit; where is prosperity?" From the day I entered prison until today the prison population has doubled. Where are the lofty ethics by which the world was going to live? Where is spiritual progress? Where is the security of life, the guarantee of those things we require for our existence? Where is respect for human life? Where are respect and admiration for the dignity of human nature? Never have there been so many crimes, so much corruption, such degeneration as there is today. I'll say now, and I repeat, that I have committed no crime in my entire life. I have not killed, nor robbed, nor spilled a drop of blood, nor have I ever taken advantage of my fellow man for my own benefit. That is what I must say. I wouldn't wish on a dog, a snake, or the lowliest creature on earth, what I have been forced to endure. But I am convinced that, if I have been forced to suffer, it has been for what I really am. I have been convicted for being a radical and, indeed, I am a radical. I have been convicted for being a foreigner and, indeed, I am a foreigner. I am suffering more for my family and my loved ones than for myself. I am so convinced that I am right that, if you had the power to execute me twice and I could be reborn a second time, I would live again to do exactly what I have done up until now. I have finished. Thank you. *(BARTOLOMEO sits down on the chair. LUIGIA approaches.)* Happiness, dear sister, is the only sound and ethical state of being. Everything else may be what you want it to be, but it will not be health nor happiness. I wouldn't know how to explain it to you. The only thing I know is that you have to convince yourself.

(LUIGIA takes the shoebox, opens it, pulls out a handful of pamphlets, examines them, looks at her brother and the judge, and runs along the perimeter of the stage throwing pamphlets into the theatre. She grips the box in her hands and some old shoes fall out. With the sound of THAYER'S golf club hitting a drive the stage becomes dark.)

THE END

The text written in the pamphlets distributed by Luigia in the final scene is taken from Bartolomeo's last letters to her and reads as follows:

July 4, 1927
I swear to you that I am completely innocent of this or any other crime. No verdict of death, no judge, no governor, no reactionary State, can transform an innocent man into a murderer. Do not be ashamed of me. The day will come when my life will be known for what it has been, and then anyone who bears the name Vanzetti will be happy and proud of his name. What does it matter that no ray of sunshine nor bit of sky ever penetrates the prisons that men build for men? I have inscribed my tombstone with the twenty years of my life that I have dedicated to achieving liberty and justice for all. And, if I am to die because of the supreme injustice of men and circumstances, you can rest assured that none of my enemies will be mourned as I shall be.

HISTORICAL BACKGROUND

On the morning of August 23, 1927 the headlines of the *New York Times* screamed "SACCO AND VANZETTI PUT TO DEATH EARLY THIS MORNING." Virtually every newspaper in this country, Europe and Latin America carried the news. Thus, after seven years, one of the most controversial trials in the United States had ended with the execution of Nicola Sacco and Bartolomeo Vanzetti.

The trial, which shook the world and caused mass demonstrations, began in 1920 with the robbery of a payroll delivery in Bridgewater, Massachusetts, followed in 1921 by and a similar robbery and the murder of a company paymaster and his guard in South Braintree. Vanzetti and Sacco were indicted and jailed for the second crime because of their resemblance to the perpetrators, their unconvincing alibis and their participation in certain radical activities.

The political climate at the time of the arrests was one of unrest, fear and antipathy toward the waves of immigrants who were pouring into the United States. Two years earlier, the government in response to several bombings, communist rallies and dissemination of revolutionary materials by anarchists, had conducted "Red raids," rounding up those immigrants who espoused any form of violent government change and deporting them. Suspicion of all foreigners lingered on; in the Boston area this was directed largely toward the newly arrived Italian immigrants.

Conditioned to distrust foreigners, the witnesses to the second crime assumed that, because the murderers appeared dark and sinister and spoke another language, they must be Italian. Vanzetti and Sacco fit the physical description and were known to be proponents of radical changes in government. Vanzetti had written manifestos on liberty and the equality of all men and had organized rallies to encourage workers to demand their rights. So, the two were arrested.

Through the seven years of their imprisonment, many students, intellectuals, writers, political figures and common workmen, here and abroad, took up the defense of the two men, convinced that the judge and prosecutor were biased and that their only crime was that they were aliens. The confession in 1925 of a convicted murderer named Celestino Madeiros, in which he claimed that it was his gang which had committed the Braintree robbery and murder and that he did not know either Sacco or Vanzetti, was rejected by the Court. Appeals by the defense team to higher courts and to the governor of Massachusetts were denied.

Controversy over the case continues to this day. It has been the subject of several books and numerous investigative research papers: principal among these, in defense of the two men, were works by such luminaries as Felix Frankfurter, Walter Lippmann, Heyward Braun, John Dos Passos and Upton Sinclair. Some other well-researched studies suggest that, despite the universal outcry at their execution, Sacco and Vanzetti were indeed guilty.

Bartolomeo Vanzetti (left) and Nicola Sacco (right)

On August 27, 1977, marking the fiftieth anniversary of their execution, Michael S. Dukakis, Governor of Massachusetts, issued a proclamation which, while it did not give the men a posthumous pardon, called upon the people of the Commonwealth "to reflect upon these tragic events, and draw from their historic lessons the resolve to prevent the forces of intolerance, fear and hatred from ever again uniting to overcome the rationality, wisdom, and fairness to which our legal system aspires."

M.-A. L.

ADDITIONAL NOTE ON THE PLAY

Luis Araújo belongs to a new generation of Spanish playwrights who are writing for audiences in search of challenging theatrical experiences in plays unfettered from dramatic clichés. His *Vanzetti* provides both challenges and aesthetic satisfactions. Based on the controversial Sacco-Vanzetti case of 1920-1927, which also inspired Maxwell Anderson's protest drama, *Gods of the Lightning*, in 1928, Araújo's play draws directly from the published letters of the idealistic and ill-fated Bartolomeo Vanzetti to his sister in Italy. The documentary material is woven skillfully into a theatrically compelling drama. *Vanzetti* also affords directors and set designers opportunities for imaginative, nonliteral stagings, and with a cast of only three, it is attractive to both larger theatres and groups with limited resources.

Vanzetti was originally staged at Madrid's influential fringe theatre known as the Cuarta Pared ("Fourth Wall"), which offers a constant fare of new dramatic writing by younger Iberian playwrights. While some of these productions are in the "workshop" stage or even hark back to theatrical experiments of past decades, *Vanzetti* emerged as a masterfully-crafted contemporary piece that can withstand the sharpest critical scrutiny. On a smaller scale, it offers the kind of theatrical interweaving of existing text into new dramatic form that contributed to the success in the United States of *Gross Indecency: The Three Trials of Oscar Wilde*, by the Argentine-American playwright Moises Kaufmann. With *Vanzetti*, Luis Araújo has demonstrated that the best of "alternative" theatre is neither self-limiting nor inaccessible to a variety of audiences.

Marion Peter Holt

CRITICAL REACTION TO THE PLAY

"From Vanzetti's letters to his family and his concluding statement in self-defense, Luis Araújo has designed a forceful and dynamic theatrical piece. . . . the bare stage setting for *Vanzetti* enhances the realistic impact of its political discourse; the authentic emotion of the three actors gives the play its humanity."

Javier Villan
El Mundo, Madrid, Spain, November 1993

"The play has a predictable, linear beginning. . . . But it grows in form throughout the introduction of beautiful, evocative passages, rapid doubling [of one actor in two roles], and the symbolic use of the simple space."

José Enriquez
Guía del Ocio, Madrid, Spain, November 1993

"The well-known social drama, of supposed guilt or innocence, coexists with the unknown, deeply bitter, intimate drama suffered by the family."

José Ferrándiz Casares
Información, Alicante, Spain, October 1994

"It's true that the play uses some strategies of Brechtian-epic theatre. It rejects chronological time and drama per se, in favor of a fragmented narration, presented by actors who frequently change character. But it is also true, ideologically speaking, that the performanceis distinct from dialectical materialism. Indeed, it is the monologue of a solitary, isolated man, fighting alone not only against a cynical judicial machine but also against his family. And even against his sister and confidant, whose own discourse shifts between piety and so-called good sense."

Manuel João Gomes
Público, Porto, Portugal, July 1995

"For the three resident actors of the Thalie Company . . . it was important to offer this production as testimony to workers' struggle." [And for Amnesty International], "Vanzetti is a symbol of innocence, a scapegoat. Moreover, on the fiftieth anniversary of the Declaration of the Rights of Man, it seemed important to us to reaffirm our position on the death penalty."

A. G.
Presse-Océan, Nantes, France, April 1998

TRANSLATOR'S ACKNOWLEDGMENTS

As translator, I would like to express my gratitude to the playwright, Luis Araújo, for granting me permission to take his words and make them my own. I would like to thank Phyllis Zatlin and Marion Holt who shared my interest in the play and encouraged me to undertake the translation. Dr. Zatlin was, in addition, a grand mentor and muse at times when I needed advice and inspiration. I am grateful also to Leonardo Mazzara for assisting with the editing and formatting of the play. Finally, I would like to thank the librarians at Princeton Public Library for their assistance in retrieving materials for me from the Internet and Princeton University for the opportunity to do my background research at Firestone Library.

ABOUT THE TRANSLATOR

Mary-Alice Lessing attended Smith College and spent her junior year at the Colegio de México studying Mexican literature and archaeology. She received her BA from Smith College and an MA in Spanish Literature from Middlebury College. She taught French and Spanish in the Princeton Regional School system for 23 years, during which time she received two summer grants from the National Endowment for the Humanities, one for Francophone Studies at CUNY and one for Hispanic Studies at Princeton University. Since retirement she has been awarded an MA in Translation from Rutgers, the State University of New Jersey. She recently completed a translation called *Blackout* of the play *Oscuro total* by the noted Cuban-American playwright Matías Montes Huidobro.

ESTRENO CONTEMPORARY SPANISH PLAYS

No. 1 Jaime Salom: *Bonfire at Dawn*
No. 2 José López Rubio: *In August We Play the Pyrenees*
No. 3 Ramón del Valle-Inclán: *Savage Acts: Four Plays*
No. 4 Antonio Gala: *The Bells of Orleans*
No. 5 Antonio Buero-Vallejo: *The Music Window*
No. 6 Paloma Pedrero: *Parting Gestures with A Night in the Subway* (Revised edition)
No. 7 Ana Diosdado: *Yours for the Asking*
No. 8 Manuel Martínez Mediero: *A Love Too Beautiful*
No. 9 Alfonso Vallejo: *Train to Kiu*
No. 10 Alfonso Sastre: *The Abandoned Doll. Young Billy Tell*
No. 11 Lauro Olmo and Pilar Encisco: *The Lion Calls a Meeting. The Lion Foiled. The Lion in Love*
No. 12 José Luis Alonso de Santos: *Hostages in the Barrio*
No. 13 Fermín Cabal: *Passage*
No. 14 Antonio Buero-Vallejo: *The Sleep of Reason*
No. 15 Fernando Arrabal: *The Body-Builder's Book of Love*
No. 16 Luis Araújo: *Vanzetti*

Nos. 1-5 & 7-11: $6; No. 6 revised & 12-16: $8.
U.S. Mail: $1.25 each, first two volumes; additional volumes postpaid.
Standard discounts to bookstores.

Send orders to:

ESTRENO Plays
Dept. of Spanish & Portuguese, FAS
Rutgers, The State University of New Jersey
105 George St.
New Brunswick, NJ 08901-1414

FAX: 1-732/ 932-9837   Phone: 1-732/932-9412x25
E-mail: ESTRPLAY@rci.rutgers.edu

ENTRE ACTOS: DIÁLOGOS SOBRE TEATRO ESPAÑOL ENTRE SIGLOS

ESTRENO Studies in Contemporary Spanish Theater 2
Edited by Martha T. Halsey and Phyllis Zatlin

Forty-two essays on contemporary Spanish theater, eighteen in English, others in Spanish. Includes essays and photos of five featured playrights and twenty-five production photos.

Order at $26.50 per copy, postpaid, from

Estreno Estudios
350 N. Burrowes Bldg.
Penn State University
University Park, PA 16802 USA